P is for Pilgrim

A Thanksgiving Alphabet

Written by Carol Crane and Illustrated by Helle Urban

Sleeping Bear Press
www.sleepingbearpress.com

Sleeping Bear Press is an imprint of Gale, a part of Cengage Learning.

2003 © Printed and bound in the United States.

10 9 8 7 6 5 4 (case)
10 9 8 7 6 5 4 3 (pbk)

Library of Congress Cataloging-in-Publication Data
Crane, Carol, 1933-
P is for pilgrim : a Thanksgiving alphabet / by Carol Crane ;
illustrated by Helle Urban.
p. cm.
Summary: Examines the history and lore of Thanksgiving from A for
"across the Atlantic Ocean" to Z for the "zeppelin-like" balloons in the
Macy's Thanksgiving Day Parade.

case: ISBN 978-1-58536-134-2   pbk: 978-1-58536-353-7

1. Thanksgiving Day-Juvenile literature. 2. Pilgrims (New Plymouth
Colony)—Juvenile literature. 3. English language-Alphabet-Juvenile literature.
[1. Thanksgiving Day. 2. Pilgrims (New Plymouth Colony) 3. Alphabet.]
I. Urban, Helle, ill. II. Title.
GT4975 .C67 2003
394.2649—dc21   2003010464

Printed by Bang Printing, Brainerd, MN, CB - 4th Ptg., PB - 3rd Ptg., 09/2009

Author's Note

Connecting the wonderful values between the past and the present of this Thanksgiving alphabet has been an encounter with time. The past gives us the history of 102 brave pilgrims who set forth and started a new life in America. They came to this country to establish freedoms not found in England or Holland at that time. Writing the Mayflower Compact was the beginning of the laws and standards for our country, as well as the foundation for our Constitution and Declaration of Independence.

The Native American's friendship with the Pilgrims was a reflection of good. The harvest meal, lasting three days, was a gesture of gratitude, thankfulness, and prayers for the Pilgrims' survival.

Today, we gather with families and friends, setting aside this day for thankful prayers. We also realize on this day worldwide dependence and relationships with each other. A moment of quiet prayer with families and friends engages us with heartwarming gratitude for this great country and our first settlers.

—Carol Crane

The Mayflower en route to America, landed at Plymouth, 1620.

Across the Atlantic Ocean,
a lone ship on a vast sea.
Ablaze with new hope,
all praying to be free.

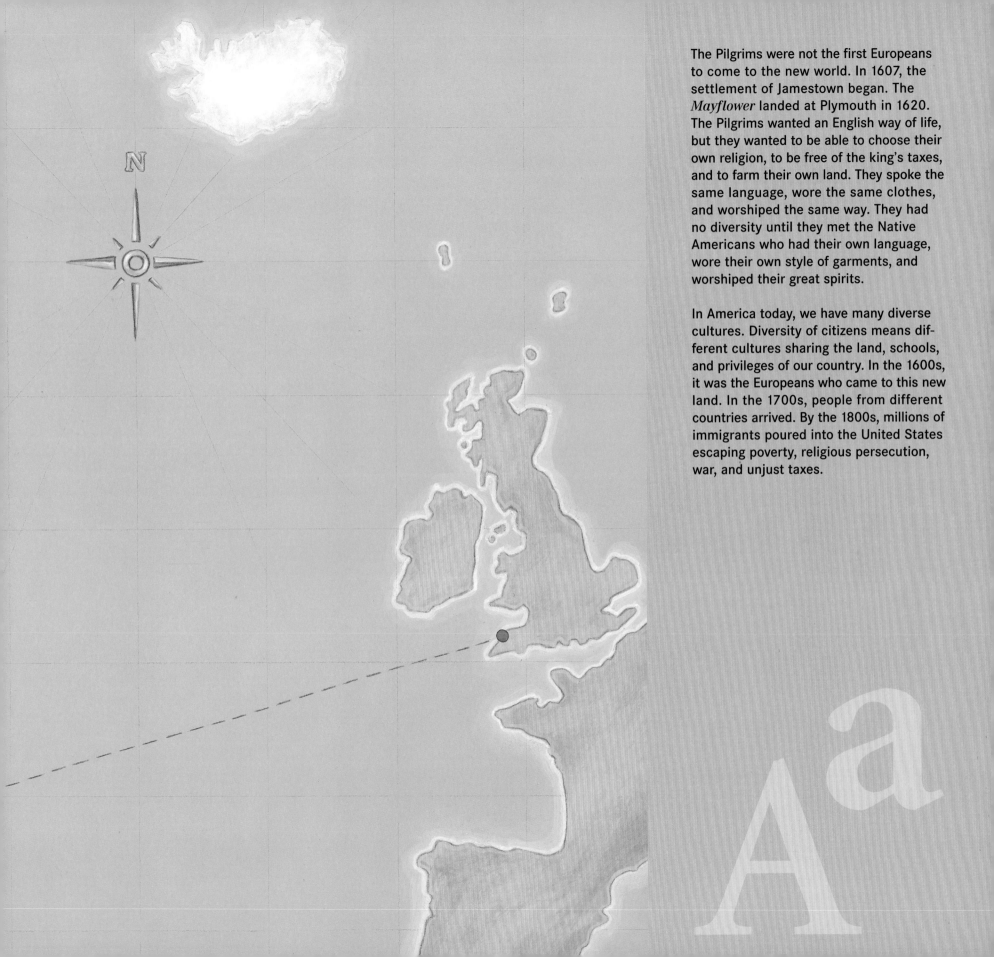

The Pilgrims were not the first Europeans to come to the new world. In 1607, the settlement of Jamestown began. The *Mayflower* landed at Plymouth in 1620. The Pilgrims wanted an English way of life, but they wanted to be able to choose their own religion, to be free of the king's taxes, and to farm their own land. They spoke the same language, wore the same clothes, and worshiped the same way. They had no diversity until they met the Native Americans who had their own language, wore their own style of garments, and worshiped their great spirits.

In America today, we have many diverse cultures. Diversity of citizens means different cultures sharing the land, schools, and privileges of our country. In the 1600s, it was the Europeans who came to this new land. In the 1700s, people from different countries arrived. By the 1800s, millions of immigrants poured into the United States escaping poverty, religious persecution, war, and unjust taxes.

Bb

The Bill of Rights outlines the pursuit of happiness for each one of our citizens. It became the first ten amendments to the Constitution in 1787 to protect those rights.

The Constitution of the United States is a model of how a democracy works. This great document is the work of many elected delegates and is an example of cooperation, dedication, and compromise. The efforts of these men provided for an entirely new frame of central government. Three branches of government created a balance of federal power: the executive, legislative, and judicial branches.

The Declaration of Independence was written by five great patriots: Thomas Jefferson, John Adams, Roger Sherman, Benjamin Franklin, and Robert Livingston. They wanted the united colonies to be free and independent states, with no allegiance to the British crown. This document was signed on July 4, 1776. Today we celebrate the 4th of July as a day of independence and freedom.

These documents were inspired in part by the Pilgrim's Mayflower Compact (*also see R*).

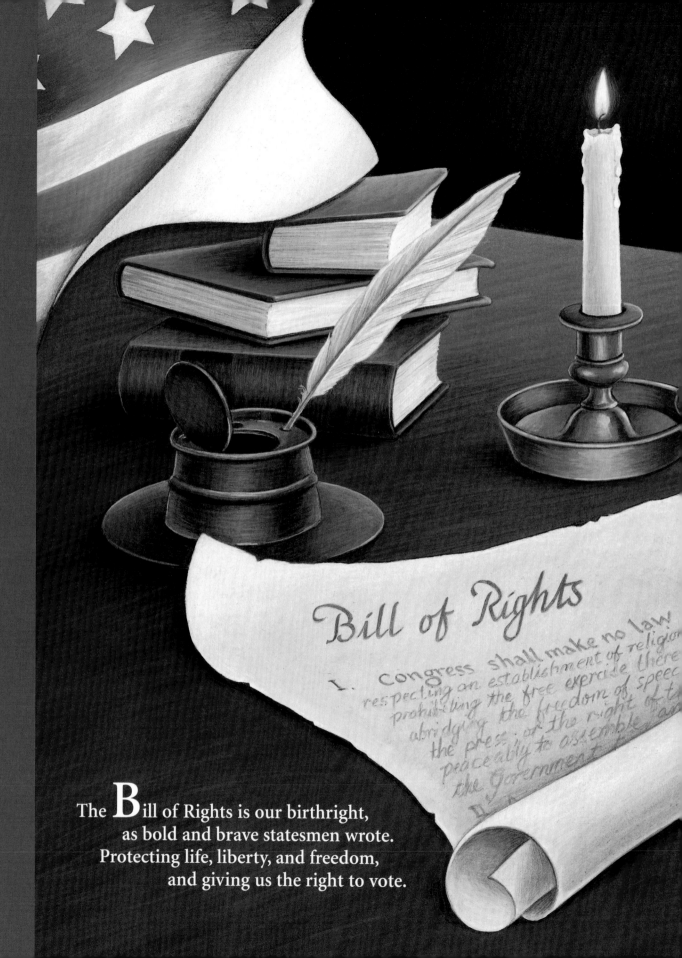

The **B**ill of Rights is our birthright,
as bold and brave statesmen wrote.
Protecting life, liberty, and freedom,
and giving us the right to vote.

When the Pilgrims landed they found a deserted Indian village and fields that had been abandoned. They also found kernels of corn buried in baskets. The Indians had left the corn for planting when they returned. The Pilgrims, desperate for food, took the corn, saved some for planting, and ground up the rest for food.

Corn was a very important crop for the people of the woodlands. The husks were woven into baskets, sleeping mats, and cornhusk dolls. Corncobs were used for fuel and were tied onto a stick and used for rattles during ceremonies.

The Pilgrims later told of their intent to return the corn they had taken. Even in colonial times, truth prevailed because we have a responsibility to respect the property of others. Today, truth is important in jobs, in school, at home, in business, and in government. Our American democracy would not work if people were not truthful.

A cache of Corn,
collected, covered, and concealed.
Cold, hungry Pilgrims
claimed corn from the Indian field.

Drums, dances, and games,
deer moccasins from animal skin.
Dyes for clothing and blankets,
Pilgrims thank their native friends again.

The Thanksgiving festival lasted for three days. During this time Pilgrims learned the ways of their Native American friends through games and dances. They played tag, ran races, and tossed stones to see who could throw a stone the greatest distance. People not only ate but took time to pray, sing, and drummers drummed.

Native Americans used a little red berry long before the Pilgrims landed. The Pilgrims came to call this berry the "crane berry" because the plant's slender stem and downward-hanging blossom looks like the neck, head, and beak of a crane. Over time the name was shortened to cranberry. Native Americans taught the settlers how to use this wild fruit as a dye for blankets and rugs, as food, and as a medicine for the treatment of arrow wounds. Cranberries, blueberries, and concord grapes are three fruits native to North America.

Dd

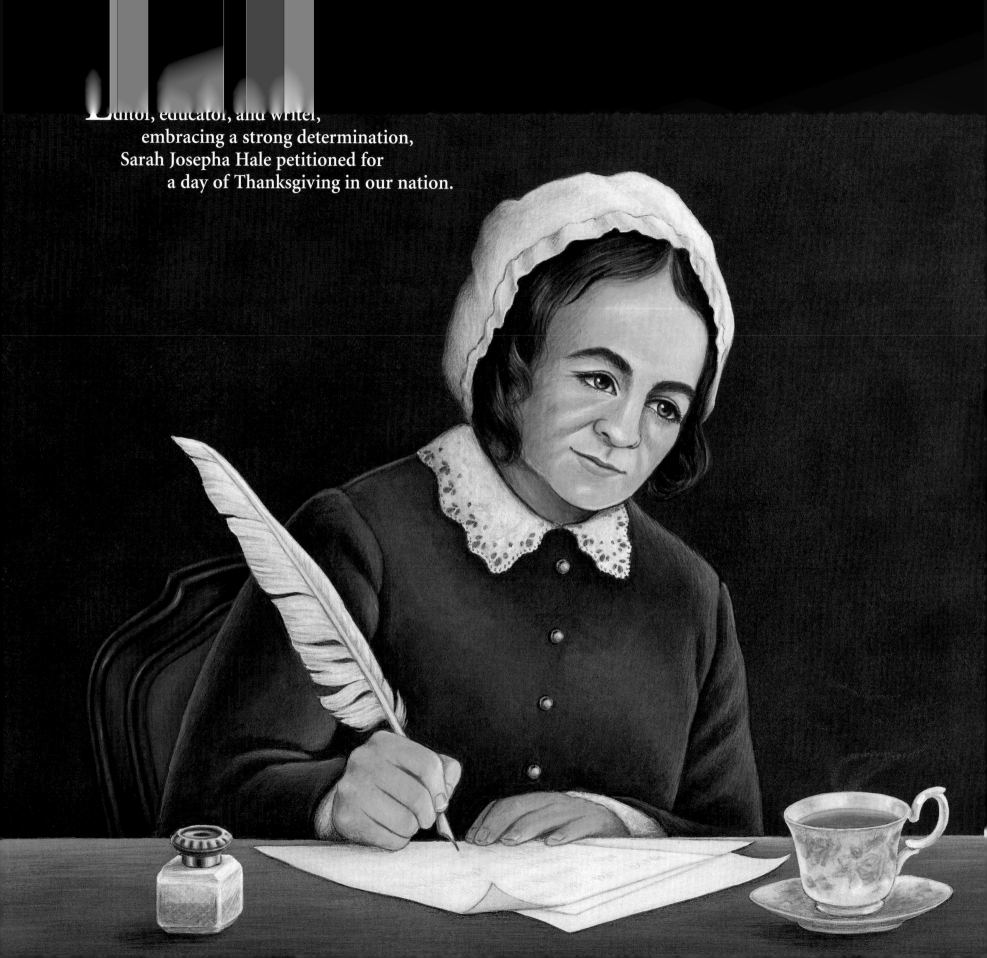

Editor, educator, and writer,
embracing a strong determination,
Sarah Josepha Hale petitioned for
a day of Thanksgiving in our nation.

Lincoln's 1863 Thanksgiving Proclamation

Lincoln

Poetry

Sarah Josepha Hale was born in 1788. She was first taught by her mother and brother and then continued to teach herself. Her husband, a lawyer, encouraged her to continue her education. She became a writer and published a book of poems, a novel, and literature for children. Over a period of years she became a very successful editor of *American Ladies Magazine* and later *Godey's Lady's Book*. She used her position to promote women's issues and education.

One of her greatest achievements was to make Thanksgiving a holiday in the United States. She worked for 15 years, writing letters and encouraging other women to write letters asking for a national day of gratitude to God. Finally, President Lincoln approved and issued his Thanksgiving Proclamation in 1863.

Since 1879, the second Monday of October has been Canada's official Thanksgiving holiday. Early Canadian settlers gave thanks for good harvests by decorating their churches with fruits and vegetables.

William Bradford, governor of the Plymouth Colony, declared a feast in November of 1621 to give thanks to God for the Pilgrims' first harvest. Massasoit and 90 other Wampanoag were invited to join the 52 remaining Pilgrims. To celebrate, they prepared a feast of turkeys, geese, and ducks, but needed more food. Their native friends helped by bringing five deer, fish, lobster, clams, dried fruit, watercress, and berries. The best way to cook deer and fowl was to roast them on a spit over an open fire. Children were assigned the job of sitting for hours, turning the spit to make sure the meat was evenly done.

The Pilgrims sat on empty barrels or together on long planks held up by barrels. They didn't use forks. People ate with spoons, knives and their fingers. All the different types of foods were placed on the table at the same time.

At the fall frontier Feast,
Indians and Pilgrims came together to eat.
Roast the deer and wild turkey,
long planks on trestles for tables and seats.

The Northeast Native Americans gave thanks daily to the great Creator of All Things. The Wampanoag celebrated and honored their great Creator with many festivals during the year. Long before the arrival of the Pilgrims the Native Americans celebrated the harvest during a feast called Nickommoh. At this time, they gave thanks by giving away food and clothing to the needy in their village.

The spring of the year was celebrated with the maple dance, which gave thanks for the maple trees and the syrup. Next was the planting feast, where the seeds were blessed. The strawberry festival was next, when all of the fresh fruits of the season were picked. In summer, the green corn festival was celebrated to give thanks for the ripening corn. In late fall, the harvest festival gave thanks for the food they had grown.

A **G**reat Creator gives
the gift of all things.
Gardens of nature,
our gratitude sings.

The first winter, in 1620, was devastating for the Pilgrims. They arrived in November and had no food left on the ship. A lack of proper food, exhausting work, digging in the hard soil, with no strong houses in which to escape the extreme November weather, and their low resistance to sickness led to suffering and death. By spring there were only a few able-bodied men and boys left to plant crops. Only three women survived and they took care of the 14 children who escaped starvation and sickness. Their Indian friends taught them how to plant corn, beans, and squash together in hills. The children caught alewives, a fish of the herring family, and put them into the earth with the seeds as a fertilizer. In 1621, good crops were grown. The settlers worked together to harvest them and gave thanks for the food this land had provided. Now they could survive another winter.

Harvest time, helping hands, and hope,
food to share and store.
Praising the land and gathering crops,
as one forevermore.

With **I**ndividual rights,
the Pilgrims' inspiration and intent
was to insure all people
what religious freedom meant.

The Pilgrims, who were at one time living in England, belonged to the church of King James I. They wanted to separate from the official Church of England. Feeling persecuted for wanting their own religion, they escaped to Holland. They separated from the Church of England and became known as the Separatists. Most of the Separatists were farmers, poorly educated, and without social or political standing. In Holland they became discouraged by economic difficulties and then decided to immigrate to the New World. When the Pilgrims landed, they named their settlement Plymouth Colony. Plymouth Rock has become a symbol of the landing of the Pilgrims. Today in the United States all citizens may worship and attend the church of their choice.

I i

Picking strawberries, peaches, blueberries, and other fruits are summer projects for many families. As guests depart after Thanksgiving festivities, many receive jars of jam or jelly cooked and canned during harvest season. Canning and preserving is almost a lost art because many families find the neighborhood grocery store much more convenient.

There were no grocery stores during the time of the Pilgrims. In fact, food was scarce. The food they harvested was made to last over bitterly cold winters. Pilgrims dried beans by leaving the bean pod on the vine in the garden until the beans inside rattled. They then shelled the beans and stored them in pottery jars or gourds which the Native Americans showed them how to use as vessels. They also dried berries in the sun.

Jellies and jams in jars,
　　　Mama singing as she canned.
Guests leave on this harvest day,
　　　jars labeled with love in hand.

J j

K k

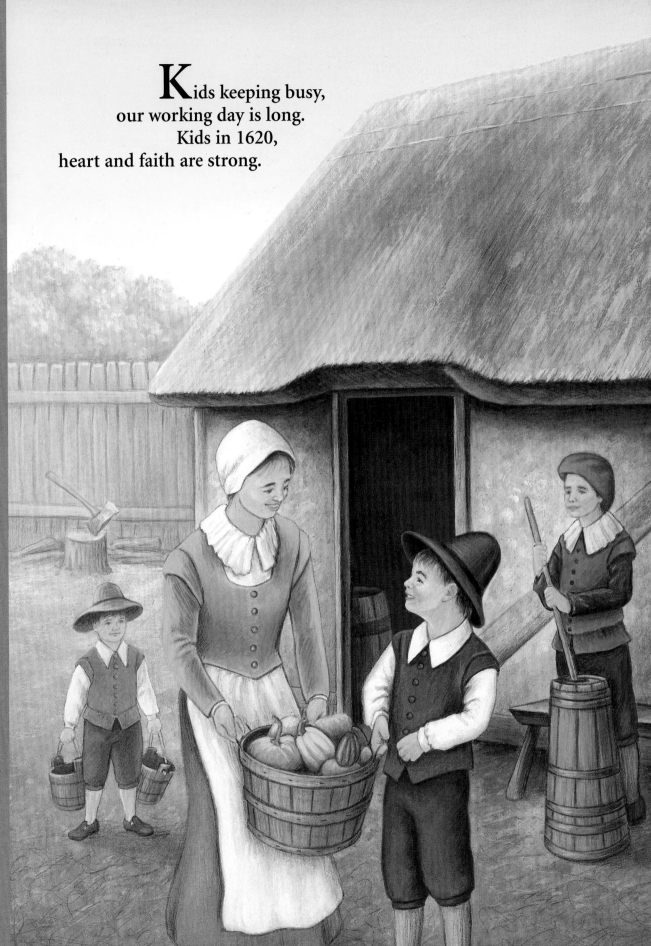

Kids keeping busy,
our working day is long.
Kids in 1620,
heart and faith are strong.

The Pilgrim children of the 1600s had to work very hard. They had to help gather berries, bring water from the brooks or springs, gather firewood, gather stones out of the fields, pull weeds, help plant crops, and help with the harvest. The girls had to care for the younger children and help with the cooking and cleaning. Children were expected to be polite and to bow to adults, including their parents. Both boys and girls wore gowns (dresses) until they were about seven years old. They only had to take baths a few times a year because people of that time thought bathing was unhealthy. Children often slept on straw mattresses that were laid on the floor at night or they slept in their parents' bed.

There was no school in early Plymouth. Parents or neighbors taught them to read from the Bible. Even though they worked very hard, they did have time to play with their native playmates.

Land, land ho! At last, America!
Our dreams have come true.
Life, liberty, and the pursuit of happiness!
Oh Lord, we thank you!

One hundred and two Pilgrims left Plymouth, England to pursue a new life, and were relieved to see land after 66 days at sea. These brave people left families and some left their own children behind daring to go forward with their dreams. Two ships were to leave for America, the *Speedwell* and the *Mayflower*, but the *Speedwell* was forced to return to England. The ship was leaking and finally abandoned. Twenty of her passengers boarded the already crowded *Mayflower* and the journey to America began.

1

Miles Standish came to the New World as a military advisor to the Pilgrims. He did not understand the Native American culture but he worked hard to be friendly and to accept their ways. As he scouted along the shore, he named their new home Plymouth after the port they had sailed from in England. He is best known from Henry Longfellow's poem *The Courtship of Miles Standish*, written in 1863.

*M*ayflower moored in Massachusetts,
Miles Standish led men to explore.
A new strange land now called home,
for everyone rich or poor.

THE CAPITOL IN WASHINGTON D.C.

A **N**ative, a pilgrim family,
neighbors in a newfound nation.
On the National Capitol rotunda,
sculptures for each generation.

The Landing of the Pilgrims 1620 was carved in 1825 by the Italian sculptor Enrico Causici. This is one of four carved scenes that are over the rotunda doors at the capitol in Washington, D.C. A Native American sits on a rock and holds out his hand with corn and friendship. The Pilgrim family is a father, mother, and child in a boat coming to shore.

Our United States capitol stands for the land, the people, the government, and the laws of our country. When we visit our capitol we can watch our government working. There are the legislative, executive, and judicial branches. Just think, the Pilgrims that came to our country hundreds of years ago carried out the idea of the people ruling their own country.

N n

On **O**cean seas, an overcrowded ship,
a baby's first cry is heard.
Oceanus Hopkins is born,
a life for the new world occurred.

During the crossing of the Atlantic Ocean, there were calm clear days and days of raging storms. A new baby was born on the ship while on the high seas. His mother named him Oceanus. Can you guess why this mother named her new baby Oceanus? After the *Mayflower* arrived off the tip of Cape Cod, another baby was born on the ship. He was named Peregrine, which means "one who has made a journey."

P

Pp

Pumpkin pudding, pumpkin bread,
and pumpkin spicy pies.
Pumpkin bars and pumpkin cakes, oh!
How they appetize.

Native Americans called pumpkins "isquotm squash." The colonists called them pumpions. This fruit became a staple of the Pilgrims. Native Americans flattened strips of pumpkins, dried them and made mats. They also used pumpkin seeds for food and medicine. Pies were not made in colonial days because they did not have flour. They cut off the pumpkin tips, removed the seeds and filled the insides with milk, spices, and honey. This was baked in hot ashes and is the origin of pumpkin pie. Today, many people love the smell of pumpkin pies baking!

The Pilgrim families brought very little with them on the *Mayflower*. They brought a few quilts to help against the cold winter nights. The early settlers were very poor and could not replace possessions. Everything was repaired again and again and this was especially true of the family quilts, which were patched with scraps of fabric from old clothing. After many repairs, the quilts took on a patchwork design. In the evening after a day of hard work, the women were not able to be idle. They would patch, mend, and sew clothes and bedding. Many of them used quills for needles.

The children sat by their mother's side and practiced their writing skills. They did not have pencils or pens like we have today, so they used quill pens that came from feathers of turkeys or quail and also porcupine quills. They used charred wood from the fireplace mixed with water and mud as ink.

Quietly quilting by firelight,
    scraps of old cloth the women sew.
The children writing their ABCs
    using quills for pens long ago.

The Mayflower Compact was a document designed to give all families peace, refuge, and tranquility, or to be calm in spirit and mind. Forty-one Pilgrim men signed this document. Through the years, our country has fought many wars to attain life, liberty, freedom of press, and freedom of speech. None of us work, think, believe, or act the same way. However, each one of us has the right to find happiness in our own way as long as it does not interfere with the rights of others. By establishing a republic, we are not governed by a king but by a government chosen by the people. Thanksgiving is a time for all citizens to reflect and respect each other's rights.

All **R**aces in our republic
   respect each other's rights and responsibility.
Our forefathers pledged all citizens
   are entitled to peace, refuge, and tranquility.

Squanto was a native of the Patuxet tribe. He was tricked, captured, and taken to Spain by sailors and sold as a slave. He was befriended by a friar who helped him escape to England. While in England Squanto learned to speak and understand English, and eventually made his way back to the New World. Squanto's friend Samoset came from the Algonquin tribe and lived near the coast of Maine. Samoset learned English from the fisherman who came to fish off the coast.

One spring, Samoset and Squanto were hunting together in the woods. They were surprised to see people from England in their deserted village. They walked out of the woods and said "Welcome, English." The Pilgrims were very surprised to meet two Indians who spoke English.

The Pilgrims were not doing well, with little food. They were living in dirt-covered shelters. Many died over the severe winter. Squanto stayed with the new settlers and taught them how to grow and use native plants and how to hunt.

S s

Samoset and Squanto, Indian friends,
two forest ghosts of shadow and light.
Stepped from the trees to welcome us,
no food, nor shelter was our sad plight.

Benjamin Franklin wanted the wild turkey to be our national symbol rather than the bald eagle. He felt the turkey was wily, cunning, and a survivor, traits represented in the first settlers of America.

The bald eagle is on the back of a United States dollar bill. There, the banner in the eagle's mouth says *E Pluribus Unum*, meaning "one nation from many people." Above the eagle there are 13 stars, representing the 13 original colonies. The eagle holds in his talons an olive branch on one side, representing peace, and arrows on the other, representing war. The eagle faces the olive branch, toward peace.

The tale of Tom Turkey, as told,
a sly and magnificent bird,
was wanted as our national symbol,
but the bald eagle was preferred.

THANKSGIVING

A **U**niversal umbrella of nations,
united through prayer and celebrations.
Thankful for worldwide blessings
we bow our heads in dedication.

There are eight nations that have official Thanksgiving Days. They are Argentina, Brazil, Canada, Japan, Korea, Liberia, Switzerland, and the United States. The values and traditions of Thanksgiving are found in every culture and religion. In 1997, the 185 nations of the United Nations proclaimed the year 2000 as the International Year of Thanksgiving worldwide.

Viva, **V**olunteers! A very special day,
the soup kitchen is ready to serve.
Vegetables, venison, turkey, and pies,
a meal all citizens deserve.

In America there are volunteers that donate their time serving and preparing food for missions, soup kitchens, and hospitals. They are working for the common good of our country by helping others. Many children bring canned goods to school to help feed the needy.

Former President Jimmy Carter promotes a program called Habitat for Humanity. This program has been instrumental in helping people help each other by building homes for families.

The Wampanoag were part of the Algonquin-speaking peoples, a large group that was part of the Woodland Culture area. These Native Americans lived in villages along the coast of what is now Massachusetts and Rhode Island. Their round-roofed homes, called wigwams, were built from bent saplings covered with woven mats. The Wampanoag moved several times during the year to be near their source of food. In the spring they would fish in the rivers for salmon and herring. They moved inland after the harvest to be where there was better protection from the weather.

Leaders in their groups were called sachems. Each village had its own sachem and tribal council. Men and women could vote and make decisions. Both men and women could enforce the laws of the village and help solve problems. The Wampanoag treated all life with respect and always shared what they had with others. It was their kindness and sharing that helped the Pilgrims survive.

We the **W**ampanoag,
observe our wise way.
As the Woodland Culture,
we honor each day.

Pilgrim women could not vote or partici-
pate in town meetings. They could not
talk in church and had to keep their hair
covered with a bonnet. Some of the
women could read but could not write
their names so they used an **X** to sign
any papers. In colonial days, men could
vote if they were a member of the church,
owned land, and could read.

In 1920, American women were given
the right to vote. Voting is one of the
most important rights of citizens in dem-
ocratic countries. America has elections
that choose who will make the laws for
our government. The political party or
person that gets the most votes will
make the laws for everyone. This is
called popular sovereignty.

Today, men, women, and children have
the right to learn how to read and write.
Everyone has equal rights.

Do you think those brave people that
came to America would be in awe of
the laws that we have today?

X is my signature,
X is how I must sign my name.
Many of us could not read or write,
the right to do both was our aim.

Y y

Yellow feather's treaty of
yesterday, yearning for peace.
Written in the year 1621,
a friendship that never ceased.

Yellow feather, or Massasoit, was a chief of the Wampanoag tribe. He was a great friend of the Pilgrims and wrote a peace treaty that was never broken. Massasoit was a great sachem, or leader. His peace treaty is simple, beautiful, and a great document of wisdom. It read that his people must not hurt our people, or they would be punished. They also agreed not to steal from each other, and to leave weapons behind when they came together for any reason. If either were attacked they would help each other against any enemy.

Do you think our president today could use this document to protect our country?

Zippy bands zigzagging down the street.
      Zebras trotting, zeppelin-like balloons afloat.
Flags flying, banners waving,
      a Thanksgiving Day parade playing a happy note.

Macy's department store has given us a tradition for over 75 years which celebrates Thanksgiving and starts the Christmas season. Today, people get up early in the morning to watch the Thanksgiving Day parade.

In the 1920s many of the department store employees were first-generation immigrants. They wanted to celebrate their new American heritage with festivities much like those in Europe. For early parades, employees dressed as clowns, cowboys, and knights. They borrowed zoo animals from Central Park Zoo. There were also floats and bands.

Thanksgiving Day is spending time to remember the past and to be thankful for new beginnings.

Z z

Carol Crane

P is for Pilgrim is Carol's 8th book with Sleeping Bear Press. She has also authored several state alphabet books, from *L is for Last Frontier: An Alaska Alphabet*, to *S is for Sunshine: A Florida Alphabet*, as well as companion counting books including *Sunny Numbers: A Florida Counting Book* and *Round Up: A Texas Numbers Book*.

Carol has always been a historian and has many heroes she has grown to love. She reminds her readers that history is not a collection of facts but the real lives of men and women of courage. She can't decide which state in this great country she loves the most, so for now she resides in Florida, North Carolina, and Michigan.

Helle Urban

Helle Urban, resident of Parker, Colorado, has been an illustrator for over 20 years. She earned her Bachelor of Fine Arts in illustration from Art Center College of Design in Pasadena, CA. She also paints portraits and murals, and says, "Illustrating *P is for Pilgrim* reminded me of what I am truly thankful for!"

This is Helle's second book with Sleeping Bear Press. Her first, *C is for Centennial: A Colorado Alphabet*, helped her share the beauty of her home state. She credits her success to her faith as well as her loving and supportive family.